After Moses, the Lord's servant died, the Lord spoke to Joshua, Nun's son. He had been Moses' helper. "My servant Moses is dead. Now get ready to cross over the Jordan with this entire people to the land that I am going to give to the Israelites. I am giving you every place where you set foot, exactly as I promised Moses."

Joshua 1:1-3

A NEW KIND OF

VENTURE
LEADER

7.25.21
Paullette,
Trust God for
Next! Eph 3:20

Olu Brown

EXPEDITION

A NEW KIND OF
VENTURE LEADER

books@marketsquarebooks.com
P.O. Box 23664 Knoxville, Tennessee 37933
ISBN: 978-1-950899-30-2

Printed and Bound in the United States of America
Cover Illustration & Book Design ©2021 Market Square Publishing, LLC
Publisher: Kevin Slimp
Editors: Kristin Lighter & Kay Kotan

Unless otherwise noted, scripture quotations are from

(CEB)

This resource was commissioned as
one of many interconnected steps in the
journey of *The Greatest Expedition*.

GreatestExpedition.com

Table of Contents

Foreword

This resource was commissioned as one of many interconnected steps in the journey of *The Greatest Expedition.* While each step is important individually, we intentionally built the multi-step Essentials Pack and the Expansion Pack to provide a richer and fuller experience with the greatest potential for transformation and introducing more people to a relationship with Jesus Christ. For more information, visit GreatestExpedition.org.

However, we also recognize you may be exploring this resource apart from *The Greatest Expedition.* You might find yourself on a personal journey, a small group journey, or perhaps a church leadership team journey.

We are so glad you are on this journey!

As you take each step in your expedition, your Expedition Team will discover whether the ministry tools you will be exploring will be utilized only for the Expedition Team or if this expedition will be a congregational journey. Our hope and prayer is *The Greatest Expedition* is indeed a congregational journey, but if it proves to be a solo journey for just the Expedition Team, God will still do amazing things through your intentional exploration, discernment, and faithful next steps.

Regardless of how you came to discover *The Greatest Expedition*, it will pave the way to a new God-inspired expedition. Be brave and courageous on your journey through *The Greatest Expedition!*

Kay L Kotan, PCC
Director, *The Greatest Expedition*

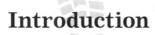

Introduction

In the book of Esther, we see the growth progression of Esther as she becomes queen and accepts her role as the protector of her people. Her life was a model of courageous leadership, the type of leadership that is still needed today, especially for clergy and lay leaders in the Church.

Esther will always be known as a change agent and catalyst leader for her people. She showed the courage to stand firm in the midst of great adversity. Shortly after becoming Queen of Persia, she was informed by her relative, Mordecai, that the future of the Jewish people was being threatened by one of the King's officials (Haman). Esther was told that she alone was the one who could make the needed difference. When Mordecai approached her, he uttered words that have echoed through the ages. He said to Esther (as she was questioning her role and responsibility as a leader):

> *...Maybe it was for a moment like this that you came to be part of the royal family.*

Esther 4:14

Throughout history, great leaders like Mordecai have risen to the occasion in tough times, working behind the scenes and encouraging leaders to fulfill their roles and responsibilities.

Fortunately, Esther heeded Mordecai's words and reached deep within herself for the courage needed to save her people. As clergy and lay leaders, you are making history. The greatest leadership stories often emerge from significant moments of adversity. The word Mordecai spoke to Esther is the word I am speaking to you today, "Maybe it was for a moment like this..." (Esther 4:14).

What is this moment? It is a moment when the local church is facing historic declines in membership and attendance. "U.S. church membership reached 70% of the population or higher from 1937 through 1976, falling modestly to an average of 68% in the 1970s through the 1990s. The past 20 years have seen an acceleration in the drop-off, with a 20-percentage-point decline since 1999 and more than half of the decline occurring since the start of the current decade."[1]

We live in a moment when an increasing number of younger people are no longer identifying with the church, or see it as a vital part of their lives. We live in a moment when churches are closing across the United States and clergy are leaving the vocation.

We've lived through a pandemic which has infected and impacted millions of people around the world, devastating families, communities and economies. At the same time, we are experiencing the resurgence of historic racism. Ideals of freedom and justice are constantly

---

[1] J. Jones, *U.S. Membership Down Sharply in Past Two Decades*, Gallup, https://news.gallup.com/poll/248837/church-membership-down-sharply-past-two-decades.as, April 18, 2019.

challenged when we see black and brown bodies killed on the streets of our U.S. cities. These moments are not easy and, in times like these, we need a new kind of venture leader, who – like Esther – is not afraid to take risks and venture into unknown places. When you see places where the signage reads, *Stay Out. Danger. Proceed at Your Own Risk,* it may be easier to turn around, surrender your leadership card and let someone else take the mantle of leadership in your place. You have been called as a new kind of venture leader for this moment and generation. I know you might be afraid and weary, because the task at hand is not easy.

You are expected to:

- Quickly scale up your technology game

- Deal with safety concerns & staffing changes

- Pastors often are expected to preach excellent virtual sermons as a one-person crew

- Raise generosity from a congregation you no longer physically see on Sundays

- Encourage the people

- Care for the sick

- Be the lead administrator; be the key spiritual guide for the church and find a new way to do church in a pandemic

If you are clergy, this probably looks a lot like your "to do" list for Sunday and Monday. I know leading as a clergyperson is not easy, but it is possible. You are a valiant and victorious leader, and I pray this resource and all of the Great Expedition resources will renew your soul and vision, that you claim the courage of your ancestor Esther and rise to the occasion because you are needed for this moment. God needs you. The Church needs you. The community needs you. You need you.

Laypersons, like clergy, are needed and have their own lists that may look just as daunting. I pray that you will also claim the courage of Esther, knowing you are needed for this moment. The church and the community yearn for both clergy and lay leadership in a time like this.

The name Esther means "Star." Her courage

was a shining and guiding light that helped the Jewish people. Like Esther, you are a star. The power of a star is special because it helps lighten up the dark night. Stars serve as a compass to help persons who have lost their way, or to persons who want to stay on the right path. If you look to the stars, you will see your place and position on earth, but stars are only visible in the dark. In this moment in our world, your leadership is shining brightly, and your congregation and community are looking to your guidance and direction. Hold on to your courage and faith; although you may not realize it, you are making history. Years from now, when future generations read your story (just as we read Esther's story today), they may read:

> *This new type of venture leader seized his/her moment, and although afraid at times, they rose to the occasion and made an impact in the world.*

Expedition Team Questions

1. Leaders, please share a time when you seized the moment and led like Esther with your Expedition Team.

2. Expedition Team members, discuss what potential expectations of the congregation might have been or potentially might be obstacles that would need to be cleared for the Expedition Team to lead like Esther.

3. As a Team talk about the openness of change prior to COVID-19, during the pandemic, and transitioning out of it. What new insights were gained as a result of this conversation?

CHAPTER ONE
A New Normal

We are living in a society that is changing constantly, hence the use of the phrase, "new normal." The changes we are experiencing are happening at the speed of light and as soon as we get comfortable in our routines, things change again. "For example, the current world issue with the widespread outbreak of COVID-19 of which impacts last long in every aspect of our work and life. We all have to keep adjusting daily activity to survive..."[2]

This explanation of new normal originates from the business world, but applies to today's local churches and changing landscapes that

---

[2] "Discover the 'New Normal' habits after COVID-19 Teachme Biz," https://teachme-biz.com/en/blog1/teachmebiz-new-normal-covid19/, June 2020.

surround us. Years ago, clergy leaders were being trained to shepherd congregations through a decade or a century, and now they need to be trained to lead a congregation through single minutes, hours and days because the speed of ministry is aggressive and always evolving. If you have found yourself saying, "My training did not prepare me for this," you are not alone.

Layperson often feel the same emotions asking, "Who am I to be called for a time like this?"

There are growing numbers of leaders in this current era who don't feel fully prepared for the tasks at hand. Like Esther, they wonder if they have what it takes to manage the new normal, faced with an ever-changing culture and society.

During the pandemic, it was common for pastors and other church leaders to gather together virtually, posing questions such as:

- What are you doing about social distancing?

- How long do you think the pandemic will last?

- Have you returned to in-person worship?

- Were cuts made to the church budget?

The common takeaway from these global crowdsourcing events was learning that we weren't alone. None of us were fully trained for this type of new normal, and we had to quickly learn how to gather information and develop solutions.

If you are like me, you felt like you were in school again. I sometimes felt like I was in my freshman year, required to download a vast information flow from the religious, business, health, political, cultural, and academic arenas, then blend it all together to apply the information to my context. I didn't have an entire semester to master the information. Our leadership team and I had to become experts within a few weeks and – the second we felt we had figured it out – everything changed. Our new normal wasn't normal anymore.

This book is a resource of *The Greatest Expedition.,*[3] and if you are a pastor, I know this resource will help you navigate your journey as you lead your congregation to become involved in your own expedition. Are you afraid right now? If so, even with fear, God is calling you to lead with courage. God promised to always be with you. I pray you will rise from any fears you are facing, knowing that God is calling you.

As you lead, consider how the texts are arranged in the Gospel of Matthew. At the beginning of Matthew's Gospel, it says:

> *Look! A virgin will become pregnant and give birth to a son, and they will call him, "Emmanuel." Emmanuel means "God with us."*
>
> **Matthew 1:23**

In the middle of Matthew, it says:

> *Come to me, all you who are struggling hard and carrying heavy loads, and I will give you rest.*
>
> **Mathew 11:28**

---

[3] *The Greatest Expedition* is a joint resource of 19 United Methodist leaders, authoring 23 books, along with other resources, to assist congregations in growing from settlers into adventurers. http://www.greatestexpedition.com.

At the end of Matthew it says:

Look, I myself will be with you every day until the end of this present age.

Matthew 28:20)

The good news is that God is with you at the beginning, middle and the end. God promises to never leave you, even in the midst of systemic racism, political discord, devastating natural disasters or a global pandemic.

If we are going to have an honest conversation as leaders, we must admit the obvious concerning our churches and ministries before COVID-19. It would be easy to blame all of the challenges of the church on COVID-19. Years before the pandemic, the Church was struggling to reach people for Jesus Christ and to make new disciples. The pandemic simply exacerbated the struggle.

I have been blessed to teach and train for almost two decades. During that time, I was able to see many of the challenges churches and leaders were facing from a front row seat.

Although I am giving many new perspectives and tools to leaders in this new era, most of what I teach has been my consistent strategy in the past, and is still relevant today.

This doesn't mean I simply dust off an old playbook and call old-school plays. Some strategies are timeless, but our natural instinct is to change only when it is necessary or when we are too uncomfortable to stay in our present situations. For instance, over the years, I have been teaching about evolving church-giving from traditional giving platforms, such as cash and checks, to more nontraditional platforms that allow members to give virtually online. It wasn't until the pandemic that many churches made the change to digital giving platforms, but the need and recommendation to change existed before COVID-19.

In a 2018 article that appeared in *BizTech* regarding digital giving for churches, the following stats highlighted how some churches were beginning to embrace digital giving before the pandemic:

Dropping a check or a few dollars in the collection plate has long been a practice at most houses of worship. But digital platforms have fast become a common alternative for many parishioners. About 80 percent of Christians polled for <u>State of the Plate</u>, (http://www. stateoftheplate.info/index.htm) a comprehensive survey of giving practices, say their church offers the option to give through a website – up significantly from 29 percent, five years earlier. The survey, conducted in 2016, also found that 46 percent use mobile app or text-based options to donate (up from just 4 percent in 2010). And nearly one-third of respondents give via a tablet or kiosk in the lobby." [4]

Although the article is encouraging, and showed how more churches have been adopting digital giving platforms, there were still many churches that were unprepared to receive consistent generosity from their parishioners at the beginning of Covid-19 because there was no emphasis on digital giving for years leading up to the pandemic.

---

[4]   K. Joy, "What Churches Should Know About Digital Giving." *BizTech*, https://biztechmagazine.com/article/2018/03/what-churches-should-know-about-digital-giving, March 29,2018.

Fortunately, since the pandemic, many churches have shifted to supporting and promoting digital giving.

Your congregation might have already taken steps to evolve in various ways as a result of the changes during and after COVID-19. If you are still pondering the need to evolve your church's giving platforms, leadership style, or systems, this is your moment to make some significant adjustments that may have been needed to make for years. For those who have studied church beyond Sunday gatherings, they have been attuned to the seismic activity happening deep below the surface of the church. Instead of the systemic activity causing an explosion of the Holy Spirit likened to the one witnessed on the Day of Pentecost in Acts chapter two, this seismic activity has been more of an implosion.

Gradually, churches across America have been in decline, and some have even died. In the work by Tony Morgan, *The Unstuck Church*, he identified key growth and decline benchmarks for local churches. According to Tony,[5] the growth and decline cycle of a local church are:

- Launch
- Momentum Growth
- Strategic Growth
- Sustained Health
- Maintenance
- Preservation
- Life Support

The healthiest stage for a local church is *sustained health*. In this stage, "Growth continues to occur not only with numbers but also with people accepting Christ, engaging in a discipleship process, and sacrificing their lives to get on mission with Jesus."

The unhealthiest stage for a local church is *life support*. In this stage, "Traditions win over life transformation. Personal preferences crowd out sacrifice and full

---

[5] Tony Morgan. *The Unstuck Church,* Thomas Nelson, 2017, pgs 6-10.

devotion to the gospel mandate. Attendance dissipates and the money ultimately runs out."

It is today's challenge to the church to move towards sustained health and continue to develop the people and ministries to focus on making disciples and reaching the community. To accomplish this goal, change is inevitable and constant. Often people, organizations and churches wait to change, and this is what we are seeing in the life of the church.

For too long, the Church waited to change or to recognize women in ministry. The Church waited too long to embrace all ethnicities in full inclusion. The Church waited too long to change and stand up for justice for all people, and now the Church has been forced to step into the age of technology. We can't wait any longer.

The current state of the church is not due to COVID-19 solely, but rather a fear of change and adjusting to a new normal. It would be accurate to say the church is where it is because of decades of neglect by clergy and laity who fell asleep at the wheel and assumed course correction would always be an option. Today, we see that many churches will never reclaim life, and sadly will soon die. But this need not be the case for your church. Instead, the narrative that could be told about your church is a narrative of moving swiftly to greater health and vitality.

In the midst of the new normal, we are seeing new miracles and the Holy Spirit is alive and moving within us, as leaders. We are also seeing needed change happening in our churches, communities and ministries.

This resource is for churches that want to live abundantly and reach people for Jesus Christ. I believe you are in a position to capitalize on the prospects that are in front of you. There is no good reason to become stuck within the barriers that attempt to convince you that you can't succeed. These barriers are real and can prevent us from reaching our fullest potential:

- Barriers of fear

- Barriers of isolation

- Barriers of lack

- Barriers of anxiety

Each of these barriers is real, and when COVID-19 arrived, these barriers were challenged by a new normal. Instead of seeing the sky as falling, I hope you can see the opportunities that are around you and encourage others of the importance of vision and investing in the health and vitality of your local church. For some churches, these investments include:

- Financial

- Technology

- Shifting ministry focus to the community and less on the members of the church

- Sharing the gospel with the world through virtual platforms to share weekly worship experiences

The need to make some significant changes is more urgent than ever, and this is your opportunity as a new kind of venture leader. The new normal we are living in is all about making necessary adjustments. Being a leader isn't easy or convenient. I believe there is no barrier that can prevent you.

Whether you are doing this as a *Greatest Expedition* team or through some other method, now is the time to launch into the vision God has before you. Together, let's do everything we can to help our teams and churches reach people for Jesus Christ. Matthew's Gospel ends with the great commission to "Go into..."

When Jesus said these words, He knew it would not always be easy. As His disciples, we must be courageous leaders, willing to overcome the obstacles we face and endure.

Expedition Team Questions

1. If you are a pastor, please share how your professional training has prepared you for this new normal. Likewise, what training has been provided for Expedition Team members for this new normal?

2. Expedition Team Members, share examples of when you have witnessed leadership pivot to a new normal.

3. As a team discuss how the church leadership and pastor(s) work together to constantly navigate and make course adjustments for new normals.

What Was, Is, and Can Be

In this new normal, you may feel you are constantly traveling between three worlds:

- What Was
- What Is
- What Can Be

The *what was* part of our ministry seems so far away, but it wasn't so long ago that everything seemed "normal." Before COVID-19, virtual worship wasn't on the agenda for many of us. Sanctuaries had more people filling the pews. The liturgical calendar worked well, Advent was amazing, and we sprinted to the goal line of Christmas and the New Year.

As soon as the New Year started, pastors and church leaders were preparing for Ash Wednesday, Lent, Palm Sunday, and Easter. Once Easter was over, we took a brief break during the summer and ramped up in the fall to do it all over again.

Those were the good old days, and while it

wasn't perfect, we had a system most pastors and leaders felt comfortable with. Pastors felt like they understood their congregations because they were always present in-person. The role of being an effective clergyperson seemed like an easy-to-navigate teacher's edition textbook, with all the answers in the back of the book.

What Is

The teacher's textbook with the answers in the back represented what was, but churches and pastors are now living in *what is*. Suddenly the reference book on how to be an effective leader doesn't work as well. No matter how many pages are added to the textbook, there are never enough to speak directly to the situations you face in your current reality.

During the pandemic, clergy flipped to the glossary for "officiating virtual funerals" or "What to do when hospitals aren't allowing visitors," but there was nothing there. We searched for, "raising generosity through virtual platforms," and like the previous searches, nothing was there. We (clergypersons) panicked and wondered why the resources we had depended on for our entire ministry were no longer relevant. And, for just a moment, we may have felt unable to lead in the new environment. *What is* has been scary for leaders and congregations because very little resembles what was. Like you, I know this feeling very well.

When the pandemic began, our church began living into our "what is" season. We started recording our worship experiences on Sundays at 8 a.m. with a small crew of people. As I preached, I looked directly into cameras and thought about the days when the cameras were in the background and the faces of the people were in the foreground. Suddenly, everything was different, and I had to find new ways to reach people – both virtually and in-person – praying that people would receive the Word of God as effectively as they received it in the past, when we all met together in person. It helped when I talked to parishioners, and they mentioned a previous online Sunday worship experience in a positive light. It was an affirmation that we were moving in the right direction and adjusting well in the midst of the new normal.

How are you adjusting in this new normal without enough road maps and guideposts? Most churches are now meeting in person (and online), but with fewer folks in the pews. If you aren't careful, you will feel isolated and susceptible to anxiety and fear. So, what do you do? You lean into resources like this. You begin building a bridge over uncertain waters and you trust, as Matthew's Gospel reveals, the promise that God is with you in the beginning, middle and end.

What Can Be

Just as we are learning how to manage what is, we have to quickly scale up and shift again to bring about what *can be.* As I follow the business and tech worlds, I see that these industries have quickly scaled up to meet the needs of an ever-changing society.

As this text is being completed, the global logistics community has been scaling up to meet the current and future demands to ensure that everyone receives the COVID-19 vaccine. I live in Atlanta, Georgia, home of UPS and Delta Airlines. Both transportation giants have built up their capacity, resources, and technology to meet the global health crisis.

A recent article mentioned the following "scale up" strategy:

> *...UPS Premier package sensor technology can monitor vaccine shipments with priority handling. It's part of a new healthcare and life sciences unit UPS launched last year, combining sensors on packages with tracking capabilities to increase on-time reliability for health care shipments.*[6]

The article went on to say the following about Delta Airlines' ability to meet the current

---

[6]   K. Yamanouchi, "UPS, Delta Prepare for COVID-19 Vaccine Shipments." *The Atlanta Journal-Constitution,* https://www.aviationpros.com/airlines/news/21160506/ups-delta-prepare-for-covid19-vaccine-shipments, October 29, 2020.

and future needs of delivering vaccines around
the world:

> *Delta, for its part, was the first U.S. passenger
> carrier to get a pharma logistics certification
> from the International Air Transport
> Association Center for Excellence. Delta said it
> can transport temperature-sensitive shipments
> across the Atlantic Ocean with joint venture
> partner Air France-KLM Cargo.*[7]

It's important to mention that these
two global companies didn't wait to begin
scaling up when the pandemic started.
While they may not have fully anticipated
a future pandemic of this magnitude, they
were preparing for something to change
significantly in the future, and they were
ready for the future before it arrived.
While the local church is not a Fortune 500
company with the bottom-line being profit, it
is in the business of interfacing with society
and helping to make positive change in the
lives of people.

---

[7] K. Yamanouchi. (2020, October 29). "UPS, Delta Prepare for COVID-19 Vaccine Shipments," *The Atlanta Journal-Constitution,* https://www. aviationpros.com/airlines/news/21160506/ups-delta-prepare-for-covid19-vaccine-shipments, October 29, 2020.

The role of the church is more than focusing on what has been or what is. Rather than focusing on what was, and is, we must shift to being innovators and helping people to see the wholeness of a life, living in the endless possibilities of Christ. This means more than developing the next best phone app. It includes churches helping to connect communities to healing conversations around systematic racism, or churches providing outreach in new ways to those who feel isolated and unloved during and after the pandemic.

As a new kind of venture leader, you have an opportunity to lead the Church into the future. You are trading your church attire for a lab coat and digital devices with the latest stats and algorithms tracking church and cultural trends. This requires leaving the church or home office and going into the epicenter of society, evolving into a cultural scientist. This is your opportunity to lean into your new normal.

Expedition Team Questions

1. Is your church currently operating from a what was, what is or what can be focus? What brings you to this conclusion?

2. Is your church leaning into what can be? Discuss your answers.

3. How is your Expedition Team modeling leadership of what can be?

CHAPTER TWO
Shift

In the opening verses of the Book of Joshua, the following words are recorded:

> *¹After Moses the Lord's servant died, the Lord spoke to Joshua, Nun's son. He had been Moses' helper. ²"My servant Moses is dead. Now get ready to cross over the Jordan with this entire people to the land that I am going to give to the Israelites. ³I am giving you every place where you set foot, exactly as I promised Moses."*

Joshua 1: 1-3

These words have been used as content for motivation speeches to groups who are close to experiencing and receiving God's promises. If read and applied too quickly for the sole purpose of motivation, however, the audience may miss a fundamental part of what transpired in the narrative leading to

God telling Joshua that it was time to make a shift. The first six words in verse 1, "After Moses the Lord's servant died..." were words spoken at a repast (meal) shortly after a funeral, where Joshua and the Israelites were probably experiencing emotional lows and highs. On one hand, their leader, Moses, was no longer with them. On the other hand, the promises of God were in front of them. They were in an interesting predicament and could have easily fallen into despair and gotten stuck on the border of the promised land. If they had gotten stuck, everything we read in the Old Testament would have been much different.

Reading this profound text thousands of years later, it seems easier to accept that this shift was automatic for Joshua and the Israelites, but I don't think it was as easy as we think. I believe it was extremely problematic because it was a time of uncertainty. When Moses died, Joshua and the Israelites were physically vulnerable to their enemies and emotionally vulnerable to their own self-doubt and fear.

In the introductory lines of the Book of Joshua, a major shift took place. God said to Joshua, "Moses my servant is dead...now go."

The specific shift was a change in leadership and paradigm. Joshua was installed as the new leader because Moses, his mentor, had died. The people and the journey had totally changed over the previous decades in the wilderness. They were no longer going to live as nomads. They would have to cross the Jordan River at flood season, then possess the promise land without their patriarch, Moses. Many of the members of the original Israelite band weren't present because the previous generation had died in the wilderness. The people and world which Joshua was called to lead in this new era did not look like the world and people from the previous generation. For Joshua to be effective as a leader in this new paradigm, he had to recognize the shift and lead in a new way. Perhaps this is why God told Joshua several times, "Be courageous." It took courage to face a new world and new people and take them to the promised land.

As a leader in this present age, your world and the people you lead are constantly shifting. The paradigm has changed. During the pandemic, I saw a picture of a church with images taped to each pew, representing the congregants who used to sit there. It was startling.

This was an awakening moment for me and other clergy leaders because it illustrated the constant shifting of the people and the world we are called to lead. You know your paradigm has shifted when you are preaching to an empty room with letter-size photos of congregants taped to church pews. As new kinds of venture leaders managing new paradigms, we have to pay attention to the following shifts:

Shift in Conversations

This paradigm shift means we have to monitor and adjust our conversation about our current reality. Have you ever been in a tenuous life situation and each time you talked to someone, for some strange reason, you mentioned your current challenges? When you reflected on your conversations, you realized you interjected your difficulties because you were hyper-focused on your problems. The same can be said for us as leaders while helping others get through their challenges:

- Loss of job

- Sadness caused by the passing of loved ones

- Anxiety of not being able to control the world which seems to give more trials than victories

In these times, we may feel tempted to join in the conversations of others and interject our own challenges. We may fail to see that even in the most difficult times, there is hope. I am not saying you shouldn't mention your problems to anyone, or they shouldn't mention their problems to you, but we have to closely monitor our conversations.

In my book, *Hope: An Advent Journey,*[8] I reflected on Matthew 1:23, which reminds us that Jesus' name is Emmanuel, meaning "God with us." When we know God is with us, we have hope in our conversations with ourselves and others. A paragraph from the book reads:

> *We are living in a season when it is the best time to represent Christ and be the Church, and it begins with you knowing who you are in Christ, and never forgetting that Christ will never leave you or forsake you.*

As a leader, what is the content of your current conversations? Are you constantly talking about what you don't have and what you have lost, or are you focusing on what you have and the promises of God in your life?

Those who follow us take cues from our conversations. If we are not careful in managing our conversations, others will adopt our language. Give them language of peace, hope, love and faith. I made a conscious decision as I transitioned through the

---

8 Olu Brown, *Hope: An Advent Journey,* Market Square Publishing, 2020, pg 108.

pandemic to talk less about my problems and more about my promises. Even with all that is happening and all that will happen in the world, I am blessed. I am blessed more than I deserve and realize.

Shift in Outlook

After we shift our conversations, we have to shift our outlook. Reflecting again on Joshua, God was able to adjust Joshua's outlook from what he had lost to what was to come:

> [2] *"My servant Moses is dead. Now get ready to cross over the Jordan with this entire people to the land that I am going to give to the Israelites* [3] *I am giving you every place where you set foot, exactly as I promised Moses*

Joshua 1: 2-3

What was the outlook shift? God did not sugarcoat the bad news for Joshua and told him squarely, "My servant Moses is dead."

Joshua probably heard, "Joshua, your lifetime friend and mentor is dead."

This was a gut punch for Joshua, but God quickly elevated his gaze by reminding him of what was ahead and not what he had lost. "I am giving you every place where you set foot, exactly as I promised Moses" (Joshua 1:3).

This was a shift in outlook; God positioned Joshua to look forward into the future and not become stuck in his present grief.

Pastors hear the very best and the very worst of life experiences in a single day. Even before the pandemic, I wondered how some individuals and families made it through their toughest moment. It was only the grace of God that allowed them to wake up every morning and press through each day. Some of the tragedies people experienced would have seemed like fiction, but because I knew the people and their experiences, their lives were not fiction at all, but actual events of tragedy and loss they lived through.

As I had conversations with people over the years who experienced loss, one of the consistent themes has been how people eventually have to move on from their place of pain and grief, even if the pace seems slow. They find a way to begin living for the future, moving away from the pain of their past. As their outlooks shift, they can finally see the sun shining through the clouds again. When our outlook shifts, we can hear and see God's promises again, and these promises affirm that there is more life to live and more blessings to receive. The good news of Joshua's story (and your story) is that God's promises did not die at the place of your loss. God's promises are alive, ready to be fulfilled in your lifetime.

There were so many reasons for Joshua to become stuck at the place where he lost Moses. Joshua could have protested that he had not been fully prepared to lead more than one million people. He hadn't graduated from any formal leadership training program.

Joshua probably felt that people would not follow and respect him like they followed and respected Moses. Joshua had plenty of valid reasons to despair, but when God showed Joshua the future (the land that God promised his mentor Moses), he refused to remain in his despair. Instead, he was able to move towards God's vision for God's people.

I am thankful that I am wired as an optimist, even though there are still times when I don't see the world through rose colored lenses. When the entire world shifted in March 2020, and our team realized we could no longer meet in person in our church buildings until it was safe, I panicked. While I kept a calm demeanor on the outside, I was anxious on the inside.

A couple of years before the pandemic, our church had gone through a tough financial season, and it took all of 2019 to recover. By the beginning of 2020, things were looking up, and suddenly the world shifted. I wasn't sure how we were going to make it through another storm.

Through the grace of God, a fantastic team and the support of colleagues, I slowly shifted my outlook away from potential tragedy to possibility. God was with us. Our Impactors (congregants) were generous people, and our ministry continued to focus on the positive as we did all we could to stand in the gap for those in need.

Not only did I shift my outlook towards God's promises and presence, but our church also shifted our outlook towards more direct outreach. We began to focus less on how the church would survive to focusing more on how our community would survive. Through passionate volunteers and generous donors and partners, we began weekly food distribution to brothers and sisters in need.

Our outlook can always shift when we dare to focus more on others than ourselves. This doesn't mean we aren't important, or that we should not practice self-care. Rather, it should not totally be about us and what we are going through, but also about others and what God is doing through them and our world. I learned some hard lessons about myself and my leadership during this season. In particular, I learned I had been too focused on myself and our church and not focused enough on others. I had also become siloed in my leadership and forgotten that ministry is a team sport. No one can successfully fulfill ministry alone.

I also learned that I needed a faith booster because somewhere along the way, my faith had plateaued. I was doing ministry out of muscle memory, not relying on the power of the Holy Spirit and God's promises.

You've heard people say, "Growing up isn't easy." The same is true about growing in ministry. Through this season, God showed me more about myself and our church than I wanted to see. Although it wasn't pretty, it was necessary. I believe I am a better leader and our church is a healthier church because we had to face some hard facts. We made the necessary adjustments and changes, and our outlook shifted, allowing us to see all that God had in store for our ministry and to focus on those God is calling us to serve.

Shift in Momentum

Once you make the *conversation* and *outlook* shifts, then you have to make the *momentum* shift. As the scene with God and Joshua quickly shifted from a repast to succession strategy, the momentum of the narrative quickened.

When God is ready to move us in a new direction, it is never feels like the right time. It wasn't the right time for Joshua because he just lost his mentor. It wasn't the right time for the people because they just lost their leader. It wasn't the right time for the Israelite elders because hadn't been tested under pressure. In spite of it not being the right time:

> [10] *Joshua gave orders to the people's officers:* [11] *"Go through the camp and give orders to the people. Say, "Get supplies ready for yourselves because in three days you will be crossing over the Jordan to enter the land and take it over. The Lord your God is going to give it to you as your possession."*
>
> **Joshua 1: 10-11**

In the midst of mourning and loss, Joshua instructed the Israelites that they had three days to pack up their belongings because they were going to cross the Jordan River. God's promise for them was still possible. It might have felt like the beginning of a roller coaster ride as the car is slowly going up the first incline and you know, in a few seconds, the curves, speed and turns will begin.

So often in our journeys with God, this momentum shift takes place when and where we least expect it, offering the roller coaster ride of your life. Do you remember a moment in your life when it seemed as if nothing would work out right? Suddenly, you received good news, and everything quickly shifted in the right direction.

A family member was struggling with a health condition, time was slipping away, but suddenly a new medical breakthrough made the difference and their health began to improve. Maybe you were approaching a large payment that the church owed and there wasn't enough money in the bank account. Then, unexpectedly, a donation appeared from someone you never met and the memo line read: "God told me to give this to your church." These sound like fiction, but I've experienced these types of miracles. Miracles can't be explained, and miracles always shift the momentum.

I believe that if your leadership and church's momentum hasn't already shifted, it will. Get prepared for God's miracles to supersonically manifest in your life. Joshua had three days. You might have only one day or one hour. Are you ready for your momentum shift? Stop looking for the right time and start looking for your miracle.

In this season, I am praying that God will give you and your church a momentum miracle so big and grand that no one will be able to explain it. I am sure the people wanted more details from Joshua, but he could only tell them:

> *"Get supplies ready for yourselves because in three days you will be crossing over the Jordan to enter the land and take it over. The Lord your God is going to give it to you as your possession."*
>
> **Joshua 1:11**

Sometimes momentum doesn't come with a lot of details and fine print. Sometimes, all you get is a few words before your faith has to be activated for the miracle that is at hand.

You can live into your new normal and take advantage of the opportunity to shift to be a new venture leader. Managing a new normal – by strategically and spiritually praying, teaching, planning and reaching – will set you on your way in your new venture.

Expedition Team Questions

1. What kind of conversation shifts need to happen for you individually, as an Expedition Team and as a church?

2. What kind of outlook shifts need to happen for you individually, as an Expedition Team and as a church?

3. What kind of momentum shifts need to happen for you individually, as an Expedition Team and as a church?

CHAPTER THREE
Praying

The first step in this venture expedition is *praying.* For those of you participating in *The Greatest Expedition,*[9] the first resource your Expedition Team received was on breakthrough prayer, the foundation to build the work of your team. There's a good chance you remember one of Sue Nilson Kibbey's examples of a breakthrough prayer:

> *God, please break through and open doors to new hopes, dreams and possibilities for our church and in our own lives...and we will surrender and faithfully follow Christ onto the open road adventure of Your new and unknown future. May Your will be done. Amen!*

Beginning with prayer makes a huge

---

[9]   greatestexpedition.com

difference. I admit, I have never been a prayer warrior but have always been impressed by those who are. One of my closest mentors once told me something about prayer that shook my world.

As he was approaching retirement, he remarked that if he had his ministry to do over, he would have prayed more. To me, he was a prayer warrior whose life impacted me and encouraged me to commit more time to prayer. Years later, I am still not the prayer warrior my mentor was, but I do take prayer more seriously and commit more time and energy to praying.

Thankfully, God hears all prayers, even the inconsistent ones. Whether my prayers are eloquent or not, God hears them. I am sure God also hears my prayers when my prayer life is less than stellar. The types of prayers that are important as new venture leaders in your local church are prayers for God to increase your capacity as leaders, along with the ability to lead in the midst of the new normal.

When I was an associate pastor at a church

in Atlanta, a guest speaker introduced me to the Prayer of Jabez, the guest was Bruce Wilkerson, the author of *The Prayer of Jabez: Breaking Through to the Blessed Life.* In I Chronicles 4:10, the following request was made by an Old Testament character (briefly mentioned) named Jabez:

> *If only you would greatly bless me and increase my territory. May your power go with me to keep me from trouble, so as not to cause me pain.*

God granted his request.

This prayer has always held a special place in my life, and I have prayed it many times. It has blessed me both personally and professionally. What was most impressive to me about Jabez was that he boldly prayed for God to bless him, "...greatly bless me and increase my territory."

Although Jabez did not tell God how to bless him, he was extremely clear and specific about wanting God to bless him. There is merit in asking God for what you want and need. I was raised to be clear and specific and never afraid to ask someone for what I needed, so this discipline has been a vital part of my prayer life over the years. Now as a lead pastor, I have had numerous prayer sessions with God that included my asking God to answer a clear and specific request. Most times it has been church related.

These included requests such as, "God, please help us to raise our budget this year," or "God please help me make a difficult decision and show me the right way to go."

Because of the Jabez influence on my life, I have not only tried to be clear and specific with my prayers, but also bold. For instance, this year I am praying that God will help our church raise $5 million over and beyond our annual budget of $4 million. I am literally asking God to bless our ministry with approximately $10 million in a year when some would doubt that we can fully raise our general budget. I am making this bold request because the additional $5 million is not about me or our church, but how God is going to use us to partner with our community, allowing us to increase our capacity and space for educational success, workforce readiness and healthy living initiatives and programs. Imagine a church and community partnerships providing the following:

Educational Success

- Extended school day learning/support/ mentorship

- Bridge the gap of transient support network for students;

- Provide consistent and reliable presence

- Reduce family transiency by building networks/connections

- Help meet childcare and continuous learning challenges

- Parent engagement, training and support

- Ultimately, positive impact on reading and math achievement

- Solve transportation issues

Workforce Readiness

- Exposure to non-traditional opportunities, training in hard and soft skills, a focus on entrepreneurship and career-building

  o Technology

  o Culinary / Hospitality

  o Trades

Healthy Living

- Enabling and empowering individuals, seniors and families to pursue healthy living across four holistic health pillars: mental/emotional, physical, social and spiritual

  o Healthy eating education

  o Food security

  o Farm-to-table program

  o Group talk classes

  o Access to mental health counselors

  o Recreation programming

Bold enough? I believe that if God makes the sun rise and set each day, an additional $5 million in a single year to make a positive impact in the lives of children and families isn't that big of an ask.

The Prayer of Jabez is a clear, specific and bold prayer. How is your prayer life as a leader in this new normal? Are you praying and making requests based on your ability, or are you praying and making requests to God based on God's supernatural ability? I dare you to pray that God would increase your capacity.

Capacity is contextual. For instance, capacity may be emotional for you and include the ability to love and forgive yourself and those God has called you to serve with in ministry. For others, it is spiritual, like a need for God to increase the capacity of your faith so you will trust that – even in a stormy season – you will be reassured that God is in control.

Maybe capacity for you is to pivot and lead in a different way, because in the past you have been solely a consensus and collaborative leader, but now you need to lead like a quarterback who can see a shift on the field, and quickly call an audible.

Much like the story of Jabez, this is your

opportunity to be bold in your prayer life. God is never alarmed or perplexed by your prayer requests. Trust me, God has heard and seen it all.

Speak out loud or write your clear, specific and bold prayer to God. Once you release it, trust. Trust that God hears you. Trust that God cares about you. Trust God has not forgotten about you. Trust God cares for you more than you will ever know. Capacity prayers resemble Jabez's prayer in I Chronicles, but there are other capacity prayers and scriptures in the Bible.

Let me share two other scriptures that can help guide your prayer life towards greater capacity. One of my favorite scriptures is Luke 10: 1-3 with a special emphasis on the beginning of verse 3.

> [1] *After these things, the Lord commissioned seventy-two others and sent them on ahead in pairs to every city and place he was about to go.* [2] *He said to them, "The harvest is bigger than you can imagine, but there are few workers. Therefore, plead with the Lord of the harvest to send out workers for his harvest.* [3] *Go! Be*

*warned, though, that I'm sending you out as
lambs among wolves.'"*

I often lift this passage when people
mistakenly claim Jesus only had twelve
disciples, all men. When you read Luke 10 and
other passages, it is clear that Jesus had more
than twelve disciples and some of His disciples
were women. Reading these words might
have increased your understanding of what it
means to be a disciple of Christ.

In Luke 10, Jesus is commissioning 72
others, sending them out into the world to do
ministry. Jesus said to them, "The harvest is
bigger than you can imagine" (vs 1).

This is a capacity statement, helping the
new disciples understand they were stepping
into a new normal and embarking upon
uncharted territory. As we battle against
systemic racism, this is a capacity prayer/
scripture focusing your leadership toward
reaching people who seem unreachable, or
unable, to embrace all of humanity.

As an African American, I have always
been acutely aware of racism and never

assumed that America had become more unified or loving towards all of her citizens. I do believe we have made progress in the right direction, and this has occurred because of people who have made great sacrifices, even to the point of death, to help change the soul of America and Americans to embrace justice for all people. We will forever be indebted to their love and sacrifices. When systemic racism rears its head in the form of police brutality, attempts to obstruct voting rights and horrible racist taunts on social media, I am not surprised because these forms of injustice have been present since the founding of America.

I find myself reflecting on Luke 10 and Jesus' reminder about the harvest. Viewing it from a sociological viewpoint of the gospel reading, Jesus was saying the world and the people living in the world are hurting.

There is so much opportunity for ministry. Each time we see racism and injustice, it is an opportunity to increase our capacity as ministers of the gospel and to share the good news of Jesus Christ. We are called to share hope and love with all humanity, including those who believe people who look or act different from them aren't worthy of God's grace and love.

Verse 3 of Luke 10 begins with a single word of action followed by an exclamation mark, "Go!" Can you feel the excitement and action in this single word? As Jesus said to the disciples 2,000 years ago and to us today, "Go!"

As you pray, ask that God will send you to a place to realize that the harvest is more than you can imagine and much different than you imagined.

As you go, remember that Jesus did not promise a bed of roses. His words of warning are just as valid today as they were when he first spoke them, "Be warned, though, that I'm sending you out as lambs among wolves."

Jesus is not calling us to easy tasks or ministries. He is calling us to difficult tasks and ministries, and you are the right leader for the job. Pray that God will give you strength to overcome every fear, and when it is not possible to overcome fear, to walk with your fear knowing God will never leave you alone.

The final capacity prayer/scripture is Paul's letter to the Church at Ephesus:

> *Glory to God, who is able to do far beyond all that we could ask or imagine by his power at work within us...*

Ephesians 3:20

This is another scripture that confirms how God is always trying to expand our thinking and to shift our paradigms to places and spaces that are beyond our imaginations. I was introduced to this passage from Ephesians by my lifelong mentor, Reverend Lawrence Young, who planted a parachute church in my hometown of Lufkin, Texas.

In case you are wondering what a parachute church plant is, envision being dropped from a plane in the middle of nowhere and starting a church from the ground up. That is a parachute church plant. The name of the church in Lufkin is Abundant Life United Methodist Church. This church and my mentor have had a profound impact and influence on my life. It isn't a coincidence that I am a church planter, following in the path of Reverend Young. Ephesians 3:20 is his favorite scripture, and like the prayer of Jabez, became an integral part of my life as well. I often close each of my prayers with this verse and pray that the same power Paul prophesied over the new believers would be professed over my life.

While in seminary studying Greek, I received additional insight to the Ephesians scripture and verse which says, "according to the power."

The word power in Greek is translated *dynamis.* The word it sounds similar to dynamite. The text is literally translated to say that God is going to do great things according to the dynamite (power) that is already inside you. That is right!

According to Paul, you literally have dynamite on the inside of you. So, be careful each time you allow the enemy to convince you that you are powerless or lack preparation and skill. You are God's chosen leader for this generation, and God wants to do exceedingly and abundantly more than you can ask or think with your life and ministry.

Buckle up and begin praying clear, specific and bold prayers that cause your friends and peers to think you aren't living in this current reality. Refuse to settle for what you see. Like Jabez, refuse to be a victim to the past, and dare to live life in spite of the odds stacked against you.

Like Jesus commissioned a team of leaders, you are being commissioned to trust God and go into a world that is broken and hurting, bearing the good news of hope and healing. You are like Paul, preaching the Gospel in the seaport city of Ephesus. You are willing to dream bigger than your resources and try harder than the attacks against you, knowing you have the power of the Holy Spirit on the inside of you that is like dynamite.

Expedition Team Questions

1. How does the breakthrough prayer created in the beginning of your journey relate to this chapter?

2. What type of dynamite prayer might the Expedition Team?

3. What insights or shifts around an Expedition prayer are occurring individually and as a team as you continue to pray the breakthrough prayer and add this additional layer of prayer considerations?

CHAPTER FOUR
Planning

After praying for capacity, the next step is to plan for what God is about to do in your life and ministry. I have been guilty of planning first and praying second, but in the new normal, praying first is always right. Prayer helps you see the big picture as you approach God with humility, letting God know that you can't do it alone. Praying first is right because we are asking God for God's plans and direction, then willing to follow God's lead.

At our church, we trademarked the term, *Doing Church Differently*™. Currently, we are saying, "Doing Planning Differently," because there is little that is the same compared to our plans before COVID-19. When the pandemic started, everything shifted. Actually, everything was shifting before the pandemic. I could feel something happening on the horizon but could not fully name or explain it. It was like sensing a storm was approaching. Maybe like me, you could feel the wind increasing, the cloud deck thickening and felt moisture in the air.

Something was happening in the Church related to planning and the planning process, and this was confirmed as I consulted and trained churches and church leaders across the country.

When COVID-19 started, I began to understand more of what was happening. I could see there was a need for planning with a focus on simplicity.

Our church programs and ministries had become too complex and complicated. Likewise, I knew that Church had become too complex and complicated. Leaders often weren't stepping back and looking at the efficacy of their programs and ministries while asking critical questions that included:

- Why are we hosting this annual event?

- Does this program reach people for Jesus Christ or divert the church's resources to fruitless areas?

- Does this investment speak to why we exist as a church or ministry?

In the work *Simple Church*, Thom Rainer and Eric Geiger make a similar observation, shared years before COVID-19:

> *Simple is in. Complexity is out. Out of style at least. Ironically people are hungry for simple because the world has become much more complex...The result is a complicated world with complex and busy lives. And, in the midst of complexity, people want to find simplicity.*[10]

The shift was literally to get simple again and take the complexity out of Church. The only way this could be accomplished was by planning differently. Here are three ways to accomplish planning differently to return to simplicity:

---

[10] T. Rainer and E. Geiger. *Simple Church*. (Nashville: B&H Publishing Group, 2011,) 8.

Planning Strategy #1: Less is Better

Live by the philosophy that less is better. In our culture, consumerism is a major driving force. Even when we have more, we want more for the sake of more.

I tried to make a deal with my refrigerator to consume the food I already had before going to the store to buy more. Sounds like a pretty easy deal to make with your refrigerator. It was a practice in simplicity and in fighting my internal drive to consume more without valuing and taking into account what I already own and have. I was acknowledging that there are those in the world with no food, and it is not wise for me to waste food just because I can afford to buy more and have room to store it.

Each of these reasons makes perfect sense, but each month I failed at the goal. I returned home from the grocery store with items I already owned and ended up throwing away precious food resources because I overbought and didn't take into account the food inventory I already had. Had I checked my inventory before heading to the store– making a simple plan – and remained committed to the plan, I could have saved money and precious food resources.

There are churches that are throwing away good and overlooked ministry every year because they operate on the philosophy that more is better. I believe the opposite.

Have you ever planned for the upcoming year and said, "Our ministry and program calendars aren't full...this is great?" You likely said, "Our ministry and program calendars aren't full, let's pack them with as many events as possible." Similar to my refrigerator dilemma, when we don't assess or appreciate what we already have we have a tendency to do too much, wasting precious resources in the process.

Allow me to offer a suggestion. What if you sat with your ministry leaders and agreed not to add any new ministry events to the calendar, instead assessing what you are already doing? Lean into what you have planned and make it even better. I admit as a pastor I have gotten caught up in the desire for more, and not appreciating, valuing and optimizing what I already had going on in ministry. 2020 taught me a lesson and changed the way that I plan personally and professionally.

As we moved into 2021, our church adopted four focus areas with simplicity in mind:

- Worship
  - o Innovative adult, children and youth worship experiences online and in-person.

- Imprint Groups
  - o Inspiring and informative small group studies online and in-person.

- Impact Gives Back
  - o Missions and Outreach that specifically focus on COVID-19 relief efforts.

- Phase 2A
  - o Next physical space and programmatic initiative focusing on educational success, workforce readiness and healthy living.

Planning Strategy #2: God first and not self

Plan with God first and not self. This is where the prayer factor assures you that you are in constant communication with your Creator. Prayer is vital. If we are not communicating with God, we have a tendency to lose focus on what really matters and what is really important. Here is a sample prayer:

> *"God direct our church and ministry to the plans that are for us and the purpose of our ministry for this season."*

You are telling God that you don't want to settle for good plans, you want God plans. When you pray this prayer, be ready for God to reveal ministry plans that you never imagined, dreamed or considered.

Most churches settle for *good plans* and not *God plans*. There is a big difference.

Good means these ideas and ministries have merit. Because a number of people in the church think it is a good idea, other leaders align with the idea and commit time, talents and treasure to the effort. After the idea or

ministry is launched, there is little to no
evaluation of the merits and metrics of the
idea or ministry, and it becomes a never-
ending annual event with a lifetime approval
certification.

God plans are ideas and ministries
that seem impossible. These are ideas and
ministries that come through prayer and
inspiration from the Holy Spirit. These
plans speak life and bear fruit. On the
surface, these ideas seem impossible because
accomplishing these tasks will take God.
Good ideas happen with our own human
abilities, but God ideas only happen through
the power of God. Good ideas give us glory,
while God ideas give God glory.

In this new normal, ask yourself and your
team if you are focused on good plans that
serve the church, or God plans that bless
humanity? There is a difference, and I hope
you never settle for good when you can have
God.

Planning Strategy #3: Community Focus

Plan with your community in mind, because churches that are healthy and vital are always looking outward to see ways to partner with the community. Some churches slip into decline because they refuse to connect with their communities, and as their communities change and evolve, the church remains static and becomes disconnected from the community. As time passes, the community grows, becoming more diverse while the church remains homogeneous in cultural, ethnic and theological make-up. The strategy for community planning is simple: get to know your community.

I am no pro at getting to know the community, especially in the new normal where social distancing is the standard, and the former face-to-face meeting with a community member has now become a virtual meeting. It isn't as easy to make the number of contacts needed to really know the community. But this is a time where leaders are called to lead in extraordinary ways, finding new methods to make vital connections with the community.

Here are a few ways to engage your community in the new normal of social distancing:

- Consider attending virtual meetings that are held at the county and city levels and learn more about the current and future plans for your area. These gatherings may open in prayer, and you can volunteer to offer the opening and closing prayer for the meetings. Also, review the agenda and see the names of community members and elected officials, so you can follow up with them after the meeting. This type of strategic and investigative work may seem unusual, but it is just the type of effort that will ultimately make the difference.

- Search for the names of the principals of the schools in your area and send them a virtual note of thanks and appreciation and let them know you are praying for them and support the work they are doing.

- Reach out to first responders, health care providers and business owners in your community. Don't make it a one-time effort: each month or quarter, send a note, email, text or write a social media post. Be sure to give them a way to contact you with their concerns or requests for support. This effort can be extended to all of the organizations and businesses in your community. Consider following these organizations on social media so you can receive real time data on special events and their celebrations.

As you focus on planning with the community in mind, the relationship and conversations may not happen immediately, but over time they will evolve. Your church will no longer be an outsider in the community, but will be a central part of your community. A sure way to know if you and your church are connected to the community is found during times of celebration and tragedy. If you have to introduce yourself and your church in the midst of a community celebration or tragedy, you and your church aren't fully connected to the community. A sign of relationship with your community is found when you don't have to introduce yourself, and the conversation or meeting simply begins with, "Hello, it's great to see and hear you."

These three strategic planning options are foolproof ways to take the complexity out of church and get simple again:

- Less is better
- God first and not self
- Focus on the community

At the church where I serve, when our plans don't align with our four focus areas (Worship, Imprint Groups, Impact Gives Back and Phase 2A), we give ourselves permission to say no and eliminate any misalignment. Even with our four areas of focus, we are constantly looking for opportunities to make adjustments and continue to refine the process.

What if you did the same:

- *Do less* better, giving yourself permission to say "no."

- Start with God and not self

- Focus on the community and give yourself permission to say no

Expedition Team Questions

1. Considering the "less is more" strategy, what might we need to let go of in the church and/or the expedition?

2. Considering the "plan first with God" strategy, does your church have good plans or God plans? What brings you to this conclusion?

3. Considering the "plan with the community in mind" strategy, how well aligned or misaligned is the church? The expedition?

CHAPTER FIVE
Teaching

The year was 1975 and Harold Melvin and the Bluenotes released a new album with the song, *Wake Up Everybody:*

Wake up, everybody, no more sleeping in bed
No more backward thinking, time for
*   thinking ahead*
The world has changed so very much from what
*   it used to be*
There's so much hatred, war, and poverty...

Wake up, all the teachers, time to teach a
*   new way*
Maybe then they'll listen to whatcha have to say
Cause they're the ones who's coming up, and the
*   world is in their hands*
When you teach the children, teach 'em the very
*   best you can.*[11]

---

[11] https://www.azlyrics.com/lyrics/haroldmelvinthebluenotes/
wakeupeverybody.html

In addition to helping to elevate the mindset of their audience to the difficulties and issues in the 1970's, I wonder if Harold Melvin and the Bluenotes knew they were prophetically speaking about virtual learning when they said, "...time to teach a new way?" Although virtual learning was not new in the first half of 2020, to do it so abruptly, consistently and on a global scale was new. I offer much appreciation to educators around the world who made it happen, ensuring our children's educational experiences were not paused or delayed. They followed the wisdom of Harold Melvin and the Bluenotes, teaching a new way.

My children completed an entire school year in a virtual learning space. Before the pandemic, I had concerns about my oldest child getting to the age where my going to her school for lunch would no longer be cool. When she started high school, we had the "not cool for Dad" to bring lunch to school and eat and visit with her and her friends.

But when COVID-19 started, school took on a new form and everyone had to teach a new way.

Suddenly in addition to being Dad, I was the teacher's helper and the school lunch chef. My kids had their spaces in the house, and we were all together at school and work. I often laughed as I prepared lunch in the middle of the school day for the kids, and reflected on how I was concerned before the pandemic that I wouldn't be able to eat lunch with them at school as they got older.

During the pandemic, teachers and students have been in virtual learning environments sharing and learning information. This new way was not perfect, but necessary to fight a global pandemic and ensure students learned and soared academically.

The same opportunity to teach a new way exists for the church. I am concerned that many of our churches and church leaders aren't leaning into this new opportunity to teach a new way. When I say teach a new way, you may immediately think about technology, but I'm talking about something else.

Specifically, we have to teach hospitality in a new way. The new way is extreme hospitality.

Extreme hospitality is a form of hospitality I have been preaching and teaching over the years to churches and church leaders. Extreme hospitality transcends social distancing, ethnicity culture, creed and religion. It is an opportunity to help church leaders critically look at the role of the church. This has long been an area of challenge for churches and church leaders. From the very beginning of the early church in Acts, leaders haven't always agreed on who should be welcomed into the church and who should not. Early disciples and apostles disagreed over baptism, the Holy Spirit, salvation and many other theological tenets in the Christian Church.

It's not a surprise that there are so many different Christian denominations today who believe they are serving Jesus, often believing their ways are best. Still, we struggle with offering extreme hospitality to all people.

One of my favorite scriptures is:

Come to me, all you who are struggling hard and carrying heavy loads, and I will give you rest.

Matthew 11:28

The word "all" in the scripture is descriptive. As the saying goes, "All means all." Unfortunately, we bring our conscious and unconscious biases as we read the Bible and process theology. The end results are exclusive decisions around inclusion, and there are people who aren't fully welcomed or accepted in our local churches.

Our vision statement at Impact Church is: "An inclusive gathering of people committed to holistic salvation and doing Christ's work in the world."[12]

It was important for us to take a public stand on behalf of equality and justice for all people and – as a congregation – to ensure that we were not intentionally doing harm to others. Inclusion for us meant practicing extreme hospitality which means:

- All People are Welcome

- All People are Worthy

- All People have a Place

---

[12] Impact Church Vision Statement 2021

In my book *4D Impact*, I wrote the following concerning the role of the local church in exemplifying Extreme Hospitality:

> *When we fail to reclaim hospitality and shift it to the level of "extreme hospitality," we literally walk away from the purpose and hope of the Church and leave it to corporate and for-profit structures to lead the way in demonstrating what the Church is most gifted to do and share with the world.*[13]

This means the local church must always be on the front line of welcoming and including all people as followers of Jesus Christ. Whenever this does not happen, the witness of the church is damaged, leaving people to wonder if the church's purpose is relevant.

Because of the presence of systemic racism, health care, education and financial disparities, as representatives of the Church of Jesus Christ we are called to focus on Christ and how we can close the resource gap for all people. If we really believe Jesus is for all

---

[13] Olu Brown. *4D Impact: Smash Barriers Like a Smart Church.* (Nashville: Abingdon, 2019), 59.

people, then we must live and lead what we believe. Accepting all people is not easy for any of us, and it surely isn't easy for me when I feel someone is wrong or spiteful. I have to challenge myself not to view someone through my point of view, but through the lens of Jesus. The words in Matthew 11 welcome *all* people without regard to race, religion, creed, gender, economic status, sexual orientation or academic achievement.

I encourage you to take the time to evaluate where you are on the hospitality spectrum. Do you show hospitality to those who first show hospitality to you? Do you show hospitality to those who only agree with what you say or think? Is your circle of friendships homogeneous or is there room for difference or flexibility in belief or thought?

Each of these are important, even radical, questions to consider, taking you to an uncomfortable place where you confront your own biases and come to grips with the fact that – even on your best day – you aren't living or loving like Jesus. When we discover this about ourselves, it isn't easy and can be quite unsettling, but there is hope. The hope is knowing we don't have to stay in a place where we judge some people and approve of other people. Jesus' invitation to come to Him is for each of us, and through the loving and healing power of Christ we find ourselves receiving and offering grace.

Through the pandemic, I have realized that life is too short – and precious – to lead with grudges, fear or regret because I didn't choose to love fully and completely. With all of the tragedy so many around us have experienced, we have an opportunity to be Christ-like leaders. Rather than offering fear and division, we can offer peace and love to all.

Remember the announcement the Angels gave, which we recite during Advent:

Don't be afraid! Look! I bring good news to you – wonderful, joyous news for all people. Your savior is born today in David's city. He is Christ the Lord.

Luke 2: 10-11

The word "all" keeps getting in the way of our bias and judgment towards others.

Whenever I feel that I have enough reasons and evidence to not practice extreme hospitality, the Holy Spirit convicts me with the word "all."

As you are examining your hospitality spectrum, remember that following Christ doesn't mean we do the base level of love. Instead, we are to seek to love and share hospitality beyond measure and convenience. For Christian leaders, extreme hospitality is the only option.

Along with teaching extreme hospitality, we also have to teach love. The foundation of hospitality is love. Without love, hospitality at any level isn't possible. As a church leader, you may think it is unnecessary to put a section in the book on love, especially emphasizing teaching love. I understand your thought process. However, when we look at the world today, love is needed and necessary, and a gentle reminder never hurts.

In Dr. Martin Luther King's book, *Strength to Love,* he reflected on Jesus' "Love in Action" through His death on the cross. Dr. King wrote:

> *We must see the cross as the magnificent symbol of love conquering hate and of light overcoming darkness."* [14]

Even on the cross, Jesus taught us how to love as He died between two criminals and in His last moments, forgave those who were crucifying Him. There can be no greater expression of love and sacrifice than Jesus' death via crucifixion.

As leaders in the Church, we do such an excellent job managing and maneuvering the liturgical calendar that there are times when we do it so well that we focus more on completing the liturgical calendar instead of fully experiencing and surrendering to the profound love the seasons represent.

In the annual liturgical calendar year, the season that is most special to me is Easter. Each Easter, I attempt to completely open myself to the pain and joy of the Passion of

---

[14] Martin Luther King, Jr. *Strength to Love.* (Philadelphia: Fortress Press, 1963), 46.

Christ, not getting caught up in the logistics, negotiations, planning and staging of Easter. I do this because Easter is the season when I am reminded of Jesus' love for me, and when I read the Passion of Christ narratives, I am invited to receive Jesus' love and share His love with the world.

As church leaders, we get a front row seat to the brokenness that is in our world as we walk with families and communities through triumph and tragedy. Lately, it seems like we have had more tragedy than triumph. In these moments, like Christ, we are demonstrating and teaching love. We are holding the hands of the bereaved and consoling the devastated. We are teaching the love of Christ as a consoling and comforting presence. When we are caught between rival groups that refuse to see and understand each other's theology, political viewpoints, or cultural values, we have to teach the love of empathy and inclusion by demonstrating the need to be in relationship more than the need to be right. When we are called to meet with fellow leaders in the academic, business and political worlds who make decisions that impact millions of people, we must not be afraid to embody the love of truth telling, speaking boldly to ensure all of God's children are respected and treated fairly. When we are called to the bedside of a person in their final moments of life and they aren't sure of their salvation, we must represent the love of grace and lead them to the assurance of eternal salvation.

This is why Easter is such a powerful season in the liturgical calendar. It is a teaching opportunity for God's grace and love. There is nothing so broken in the world that love cannot heal and mend. As you are walking through the post-pandemic period with those who struggle with loving and understanding love, continue to teach them about Jesus' sacrifice on the cross and how He loved them. He loved them so much that He died for them. Whenever we truly love like Christ, we will be able to offer extreme hospitality to others and our world on earth will look more like heaven above.

Expedition Team Questions

1. Describe how you individually practice extreme hospitality.

2. What is a growing edge for how you could practice a more extreme hospitality?

3. How would you rate your congregation on practicing extreme hospitality? Expedition Team? What are the growing edges for each?

CHAPTER SIX
Reaching

Congratulations! You are now at the final and most impactful point of being a new kind of venture leader. The next step is *evangelism,* which is *reaching.* The Matthew 28 text quoted at the beginning of the book, reassuring us of Jesus' presence, is a dual statement. On one hand, it is the assurance of Jesus' protection and love forever. This is the blessed assurance spoken of in the famous hymn of the Church. On the other hand, it is a statement issuing a challenge:

> *Therefore, go and make disciples of all nations, baptizing them in the name of the Father and of the Son and of the Holy Spirit...*
>
> **Matthew 28:19**

Jesus never gives us the easy evangelism

assignments where we show up, proclaim Jesus is Lord and everyone is magically open to salvation. Often, our experiences are the opposite. We go into places where people are not only in opposition to the gospel; they are also in opposition to you as a person. It is possible that they aren't receptive to receiving the gospel from you because of your culture, gender or family of origin. They refuse the gospel because they can't make it align with the person speaking the truth to them, so they miss a great opportunity to hear about the love of Jesus. Not only is it a challenge to present the gospel to people who may not agree with you – or even like you – but it is also a challenge to take the gospel to all the world. In the early Christian Church, the known world was a much smaller place, yet something tells me that Jesus knew the world was much bigger than the imaginations of these early disciples.

We have a responsibility to go into all the world and reach people for Jesus Christ, even in the midst of a pandemic. I am not encouraging you to shrug off the wisdom of science and health care providers, or to put yourself in danger. I am saying the challenge Jesus gave 2,000 years ago is still real today. So, the question is, "How do we reach people in the new normal where the impact of the pandemic will be with us for the foreseeable future?"

First, commit (or recommit) to technology platforms that allow you to virtually reach the broadest number of people. A good first step is to ensure that your church has a working basic website. The pandemic taught us that audiences aren't looking for pros, but presence. One of the best forms of presence during a pandemic is digital. Years ago, we discovered that potential parishioners don't scout out our churches initially by walking through our beautiful mahogany or glass doors. They initially scout out our churches via our websites or social media, and if the church doesn't have a website, the church doesn't exist for some of these potential parishioners.

The bottom line encouragement for you today is to get a basic and functional website online for your church, if you don't already have one. Your website should be designed to answer the questions a first-time visitor might have such as:

- Location

- Experience time

- Resources for children

- What to expect during the first visit

- Other information about your church that you feel is vital

We live in the bubble of our local churches, and we expect others to live in the same bubble, but they don't live there and don't get it. We have to do everything we can to ensure we are meeting and exceeding the needs of parishioners and guests.

As we highlight this step of heaving a website, keep in mind that one of the low hanging fruit opportunities churches neglect is simply scanning the website frequently for out-of-date information. For instance, remove events that have already happened, or a volunteer or staff member's picture on the homepage who is no longer serving or working at the church.

Your church's website doesn't have to be award-winning, but it does need to be inviting, helping first-time visitors – as well as current parishioners – see what is important in the life of the church. Your website is one of the most powerful tools you have to fulfill the Matthew 28 commission to go into all the world.

Another way to reach people through technology is by ensuring you can broadcast your sermons and worship experiences using as many virtual platforms as possible:

- Your church website

- Facebook Live

- YouTube

- Other streaming services

Even if you can't show the video version of the sermon, make sure audio is available. When our church first launched into the virtual worship space, we weren't able to show videos, only audio. We later upgraded to video, and now people around the world can watch our sermons live and on demand. It is wonderful to see the statistics and testimonies from our global community about how our ministry is blessing them and keeping them connected to Christ. Statistically, our online viewership doubled and tripled at times during the pandemic. It would be easy to say this was an expected increase due to church buildings being temporarily closed, but that analysis is too quick and too shallow. After a deeper analysis, it wasn't being able to stream sermons at the beginning of the pandemic that solely doubled and tripled our number of viewers. It was our historic investment in technology and in building a culture that made it okay to watch church online.

In addition, we built an online following of those who evangelized on behalf of the church, by sharing sermon links and resources with others. As our online viewership numbers dramatically increased, we could see the fulfillment of a historic investment strategy.

My encouragement to you is that it is not too late to share your church sermons and worship online. The sooner you begin doing it, the better off your church will be in the long run. When COVID-19 is no longer considered a pandemic, there are members of your church who may never return to the building for in-person worship as long as a virtual option is offered. I hope you don't look at their decisions negatively, but know that due to health concerns, it isn't wise for some parishioners to return. Frankly, some of them may have discovered that virtual worship is just as impactful as in-person worship. Going forward, the best strategy is to build yourworship experiences on in-person and online platforms that ensure you can always reach the greatest number of people.

The pre-pandemic church is gone, and the post-pandemic church is here to stay. We have to do all we can as a new kind of venture leader and as congregations to fulfill the Great Commission.

The final step in reaching people isn't technology, but will impact your technology approach and platforms. This step is *authenticity.* To be authentic means you are real and honest about who you are and where you are at any point in time. When I saw major corporations broadcasting commercials during the pandemic, I noticed more authenticity in their approach. Less bells and whistles and less fancy appeals to customers to purchase their products. I also saw less spectacular technology enhancements in video. Commercials looked as if they were shot on smartphones. These were often ads for major corporations.

A lesson I learned, especially as a worship video broadcast perfectionist, is that people really wanted authenticity in what they saw, not perfection. As a perfectionist, I can see a camera shot that wasn't well timed or a prop misplaced, but the viewing audience sees worship and an effort by the local church to help them stay connected to God.

As I talked to viewers during the pandemic and learned of some of their hardships, my point of view changed. I began to focus more on the authenticity in worship and not on how well a song or sermon was presented. Perfect worship is an ideal that can never be achieved. The true goal is to offer hope, joy and love to those who are watching. Being authentic means that you are okay with yourself and knowing that your purpose, in part, is to help others see God's grace in their lives.

The word "grace" has helped me understand time and time again that I am formed from clay and don't always get it right. It reminds me that God loves me even with my growing edges. As a new kind of venture leader, you may be tempted to think it is all about you and what you can do. It is not. It is all about God and what God is doing through you.

A few years ago, I was a guest speaker

at an event. As I was preparing to speak, I noticed the music stands the worship leaders were using had little sticky notes on them so singers could read the notes as they sang. I was blown away by the words of encouragement on each note and felt it was a wonderful idea for someone to write a note of encouragement for each worship leader, reminding them of their call and purpose in God. These notes were written on inexpensive sheets of paper, but the depth of the texts written was priceless. What if those who lead worship took this example to heart each time they shared in worship?

Initially, I don't recommend you write sticky notes to each other, but write a note to yourself and place it wherever you will be leading worship. Consider writing the following, "God, you shaped me from clay, and I am made in your image. Give me strength to be myself and inspire others through my life."

It will feel good to write those words because it gives you permission to be authentically you. Whether the music team was on point, the graphics transitioned well, the liturgist was excellent, or the sermon was impactful, will all be secondary whenever we dare to be ourselves in worship. What is primary is that you showed up at worship and the Holy Spirit used you to bless someone's life.

Let me share one more way to reach people in this new normal...through *collaborative partnerships.* I know I just spent an entire section encouraging you to be authentically you. Now, let me encourage you to be authentically *we.*

In chapter 3, we talked about prayer. I mentioned that one of my mentors said if he had his ministry to do all over again, he would have prayed more. The same is true for me, but I would add one additional item. I would not have done so much of my ministry alone. Preparing sermons alone. Planning ministry alone. Dreaming and visioning alone. Going through difficult moments alone because I felt no one would understand or care.

Ministry is great, but there are moments that can be very lonely, especially if we isolate ourselves and create a narrative that no one out there can identify with what we are going through or are unwilling to help.

Even though I chose to do much of my ministry alone, this was not the model Jesus shows us, especially since he had more than 12 disciples. Jesus' ministry was a team sport. He taught us to bring diverse groups of people together to feed multitudes, heal the sick and restore faith to those who had lost their faith. The Jesus model of ministry is one that we have to embrace in this new normal. We must seek out collaborative partnerships and stop believing that we have to do it all by ourselves.

The power of the Holy Spirit that is at work within you is also at work within others. Wouldn't it be a great show of faith and teamwork to work with others who have the same power that you possess? When we understand this principle, barriers and silos in ministry are removed. In fact, this is the primary motivator of brining together the Expedition Team to take this journey towards a new expedition together.

The church I serve has worked hard to break down barriers and silos and have committed to developing collaborative partnerships. Each week, a few of us gather virtually to hear the sermons of those who will be preaching the upcoming Sunday. During our weekly staff meetings, each team leader shares visions and plans. Afterwards, team members have an opportunity to ask questions or present challenges.

We formed eight diverse teams to focus on several key areas in the life of the church to prevent silos and to encourage collaboration. On some of these teams, members may not be experts in the area of their team focus, but are experts in collaboration and presenting ideas that no one else in the group may have thought about.

We are also extending this philosophy

to our Outreach ministry. After working with many churches over my career, I've seen outreach duplication with sister congregations more often than not. The end result was that neither of the churches were knocking the ball out of the park because they were each trying to do the same outreach. Although their efforts were admirable, they were not optimizing their opportunities to offer unique services to those in need. I encourage churches and church leaders to partner with sister congregations and cease duplicating efforts. If a congregation near yours has an awesome food distribution ministry, partner with them instead of launching your own food distribution ministry. If your congregation is starting a clothing ministry, reach out to other churches and see if they are willing to collaborate and partner with your church.

The Kingdom of God is filled with like-minded people who are led by the power of the Holy Spirit. Too often we don't take advantage of the unique gifts God has given us. As leaders on a new venture, we have to model and demonstrate collaboration to our congregation and ministry teams, by building a culture that embraces it. Our new normal demands that we work together. Church leaders and churches that are isolated will not be able to thrive in this new reality and will fail to optimize the opportunities before them.

Jesus was right: the harvest is plentiful, and there are more people than any one church can reach. But together, we can reach the world and fulfill the Great Commission through technology, authenticity and creative partnerships. This is a time to evaluate everything from the way you lead to the way you reach people for Jesus Christ. After a time of evaluation, give yourself and your church permission to change.

Expedition Team Questions

1. How has your church embraced technology as a tool for ministry? What are your growing edges?

2. As ministry leaders, how would you each take a next step in being vulnerable to offer authenticity at its deepest levels?

3. How are you embracing a collaborative spirit individually, as an Expedition Team and as a congregation?

CHAPTER SEVEN
Closing Thoughts

As you are maneuvering your new normal, consider the following closing thoughts for your journey.

Flexible

Stay flexible even when it is not easy. Due to the stress and responsibility of ministry, we can become rigid, pessimistic and fail to see the opportunities in front of us. A mark of great leadership is flexibility, being able to make adjustments when necessary. I was blessed as a pre-teen to spend several years in gymnastics training and enjoyed every bit of it, except for the stretching part. I loved the comradery, learning new tumbling exercises and performing in our local town parade.

I wasn't so fond of the warm up stretching routine that preceded all of the things I loved about gymnastics. But, as I got older I realized that the only way I could elevate my gymnastics skills was to spend the necessary time to stretch my body and my muscles so I would be flexible during the events.

Long past my gymnastics days, stretching has become a metaphor for my life, especially as a leader. Throughout the years, life has stretched me near a breaking point many times. Personally, I have been stretched as a father, friend and leader. Professionally, I have been stretched to trust our team, believing that together we would make it through the pandemic and the church would be stronger in the end. All of the stretching I have done has made me more flexible and better able to adjust when needed.

As you read this, I hope you don't think I consider myself perfect, or that I have this stretching and flexibility process down to a perfect science. Trust me, I don't. Like the pre-teen complaining during my gymnastics warm-up time, I am now an adult and I still complain when life stretches me. Through it all, though, I have become a more flexible leader, better able to cope with changes in my life and in the world.

I believe you are more flexible than you think. I believe all of the stretching you have been doing your entire life has made you stronger and that strength and flexibility is being called on for this season. Complain if you must, but know that God has given you flexibility and strength so the vision for your life and your church can come to pass.

I hope you stretch your muscles related to trust. Don't do ministry alone or in a silo. Trust that your team – and even those you haven't met yet – are able to work together to get the job done. Trust that God has not run out of resources and will always bless you, even when time is running out on the clock.

Trust that the greatest show of flexibility is leading with humility, being able to admit that you don't have all of the answers. Trust that the plans that you put in place may need to be adjusted from good plans to God plans. This is your opportunity to flexible and watch the power of God continue to move in your life and church.

Focused

Second, stay focused. One of my favorite scriptures is from the Psalmist:

I will lift up mine eyes unto the hills, from whence cometh my help.

Psalm 121:1 KJV

As you know, the Psalms are inspirational hymns that express the highs and lows of life. I have always appreciated the writer's blunt honesty around topics of fear, sickness, enemies and failure. I have also appreciated when the writer reminds me that I have a choice. Maybe this is why I like Psalm 121 so much. The writer makes a choice to look up and stay focused on God and not the world.

In this new normal, you will be constantly challenged to stay focused in the midst of distractions and detours placed in front of you.

Sometimes people may be the distraction and detour. It is time to develop a deeper prayer life and ability to discern the right peoople, so you can spend as much time with people who will help you fulfill the vision God has given you.

There may be times when you are the distraction and detour. During these moments, you have to speak to yourself and reclaim your faith, joy and peace, pressing forward even when everything inside you is telling you to stop. Whether your distractions and detours are internal or external, you will have to make good choices every day and, like the psalmist, look up to God, who is guiding you and keeping you every step of the way.

Grateful

Finally, keep an attitude of gratitude. I realize that I am blessed more than I deserve. With this in mind, it's important that I spend time focused on my blessings, not on the things that haven't worked out in my life.

Even on my worst day, I am blessed more

than I deserve. As I am writing, it is foggy outside my window and the fog seems so much like our life experiences, creating a cloudy or haze-like effect that threatens to dampen our joy. If we aren't careful, we can begin to think the fog is permanent. We may also forget that behind the fog is a bright sun and, eventually, the power of the sun will burn the fog and haze away. The months, now years, since I first heard the phrase *COVID-19* have taught me to be grateful in all circumstances, including those circumstances that are like a cloudy and foggy day. I know the sun is still shining and the Son is always with me, so I am always blessed.

An attitude of gratitude is not developed instantly, but over time as we dare ourselves to see God's goodness and beauty in all of creation. When we are flexible, focused and grateful, we more readily see God's Kingdom and Glory on earth. God's Kingdom is here right now, and it is within us – if we choose to see it – not allowing the world or our circumstances to convince us that the clouds and fog are permanent. They aren't. They are only temporary.

Thank you for answering the call to do all you can to be a spectacular venture leader in this season and in seasons to come. May God continue to richly bless you.

Expedition Team Questions

1. What is your next step in deepening your flexibility?

2. What is your next step in deepening your attitude of gratitude?

3. What is your next step in deepening your focus?

What is The Greatest Expedition?

The Greatest Expedition is a congregational journey for churches, charges, or cooperative parishes led by a church Expedition Team of 8-12 brave pioneering leaders. The purpose of The Greatest Expedition is to provide an experience for Expedition Teams to explore their local context in new ways to develop new MAPS (ministry action plans) so you are more relevant and contextual to reach new people in your community. Updated tools and guides are provided for the church's Expedition Team. Yet, it is a "choose your own adventure" type of journey.

The tools and guides will be provided, but it is up to the church's Expedition Team to decide which tools are needed, which tools just need sharpening, which tools can stay in their backpack to use at a later time, what pathways to explore, and what pathways to pass.

The Greatest Expedition provides a new lens and updated tools to help your Expedition Team explore and think about being the church in different ways. Will your Expedition Team need to clear the overgrown brush from a once known trail, but not recently traveled? Or will the Expedition Team need to cut a brand new trail with their new tools? Or perhaps, will the Team decide they need to move to a completely fresh terrain and begin breaking ground for something brand new in a foreign climate?

Registration is open and Expedition Teams are launching!

greatestexpedition.com

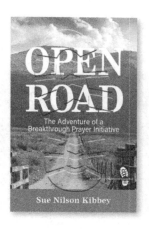

OPEN ROAD
The Adventure of a
Breakthrough Prayer Initiative

Sue Nilson Kibbey

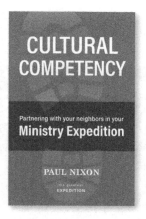

CULTURAL COMPETENCY

Partnering with your neighbors in your
Ministry Expedition

PAUL NIXON
the greatest
EXPEDITION

EXPANDING THE EXPEDITION

through
Church Partnerships

CHRISTIAN COON
the greatest
EXPEDITION

THE JOURNEY'S CALL

Returning to Our
Pioneer Roots

PHIL MAYNARD
the greatest
EXPEDITION

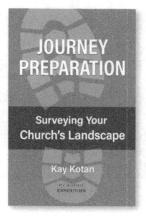

JOURNEY PREPARATION

Surveying Your
Church's Landscape

Kay Kotan
the greatest
EXPEDITION

HOPE
An Advent Journey

OLU BROWN

marketsquarebooks.com

Made in the USA
Columbia, SC
28 June 2021

40999875R00075